Grade 4th
Phase II

For MorMor, Blenda, and Trae

M. Evans and Company titles are distributed in
the United States by the J.B. Lippincott Company,
East Washington Square, Philadelphia, Pa. 19105;
and in Canada by McClelland & Stewart Ltd.,
25 Hollinger Road, Toronto M4B 3G2, Ontario

Copyright © 1973 by John S. Marr, M.D.
Illustrations copyright © by M. Evans and Company
All rights reserved under International and Pan American Copyright Conventions
Library of Congress Catalog Card Number: 72-85647
Manufactured in the United States of America
ISBN 0-87131-053-8
9 8 7 6 5 4 3 2

Every day your body has to make new muscle, new skin, new bone, new hair, new blood, and new tissue. This is because billions of cells in all parts of your body are used up every day. Your body uses the food you eat to replace these used-up cells.

Your body also uses the food you eat to create energy. Energy is what makes your body work. You probably think of energy as what you need to make your arms and legs move. But energy also makes your heart beat and your lungs breathe.

Energy makes every part of your body do its own special work.

Good food is anything you eat that can be used by your body to replace used-up cells or to make energy. The ingredients in food which do these jobs are called nutrients. Regardless of what many people believe, any food is good for you if it contains a nutrient that your body can use. Even chocolate cake can be good for you if it contains a nutrient that you need. You don't even have to drink milk to stay healthy if you get the nutrients that are in milk from some other foods.

1 CARBOHYDRATES
2 FATS
3 PROTEINS
4 VITAMINS
5 MINERALS
6 WATER

Six kinds of nutrients are needed by the body. They are carbohydrates (car-bow-HI-drayts), fats, proteins (PRO-teens), vitamins, minerals, and water. These six nutrients are usually mixed together in the various types of food we eat. Once you understand what each of these nutrients does in your body, you will be able to use the chart at the end of this book to plan your own meals.

1. Carbohydrates are made up of different types of sugar that are linked together in strings. The tiny sugar strings can join

CARBOHYDRATES

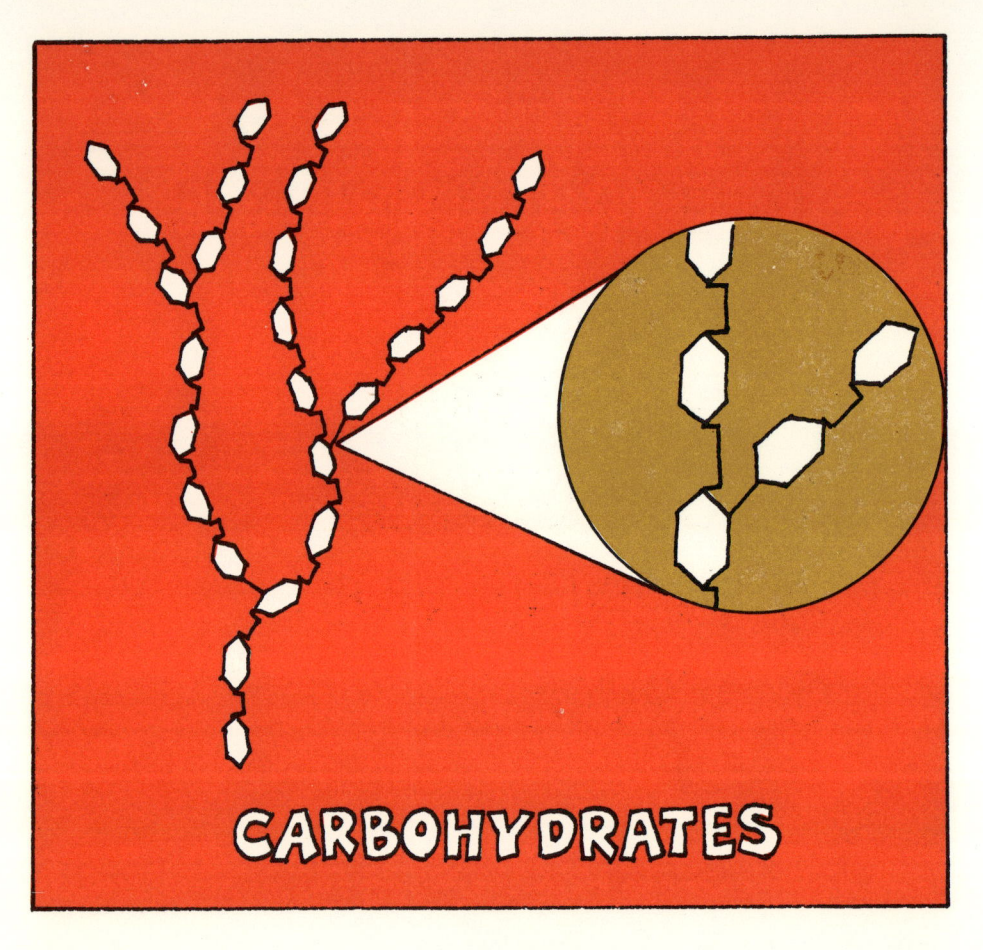

together to form a larger particle that looks like a woven net. This large type of carbohydrate particle made up of woven strings of small sugars is called a starch. A starch particle is so small that it is difficult to see even with the most powerful microscope.

The body can turn sugars into energy very quickly. But when a person eats a food made up of starch (like a potato), the starch must be broken down into sugar before the body can turn it into energy. The process that breaks down large

FATS

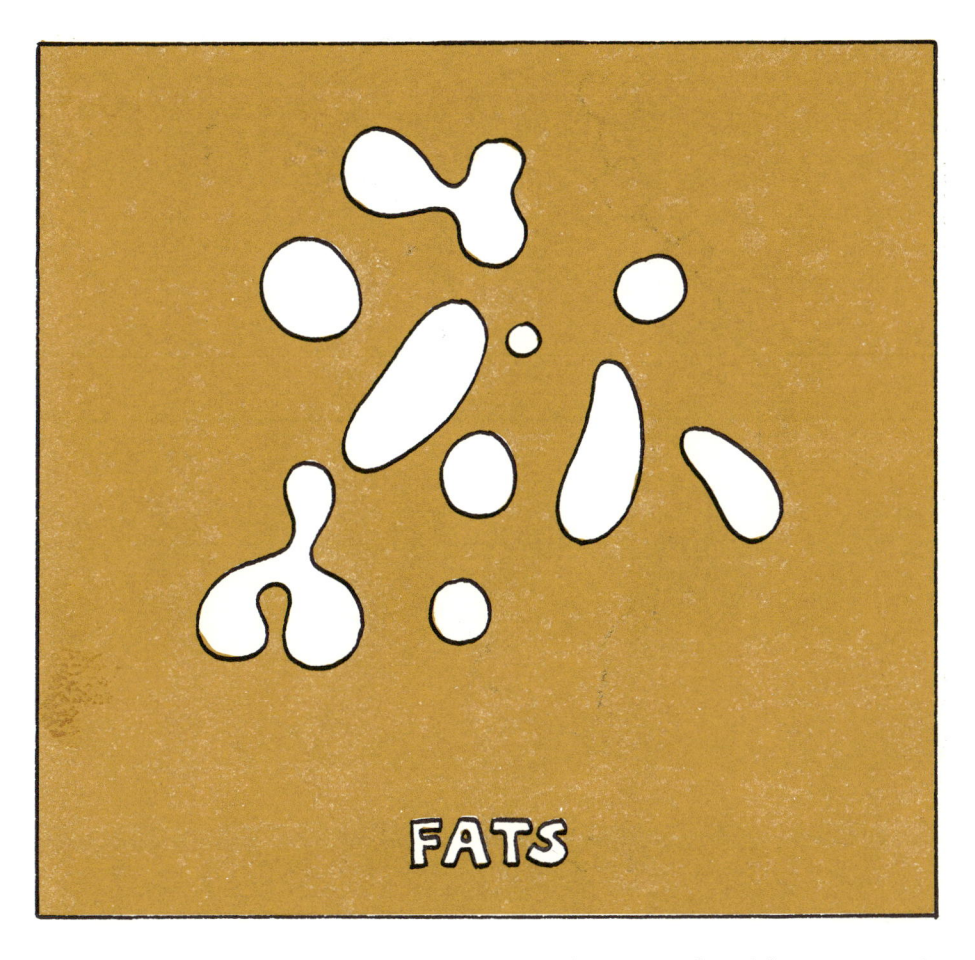

food particles like starch into simple particles like sugars is called digestion.

2. Fats are made up of a different type of tiny particle called a glyceride (GLISS-er-ide). Glycerides come in many different sizes which are mixed together to form different kinds of fats. Mixtures of very small glyceride particles take the form of liquids called oils. Mixtures of larger glyceride particles take the form of soft solids like butter or margarine. Other mixtures of large glyceride particles form hard fat in meat or wax.

PROTEINS

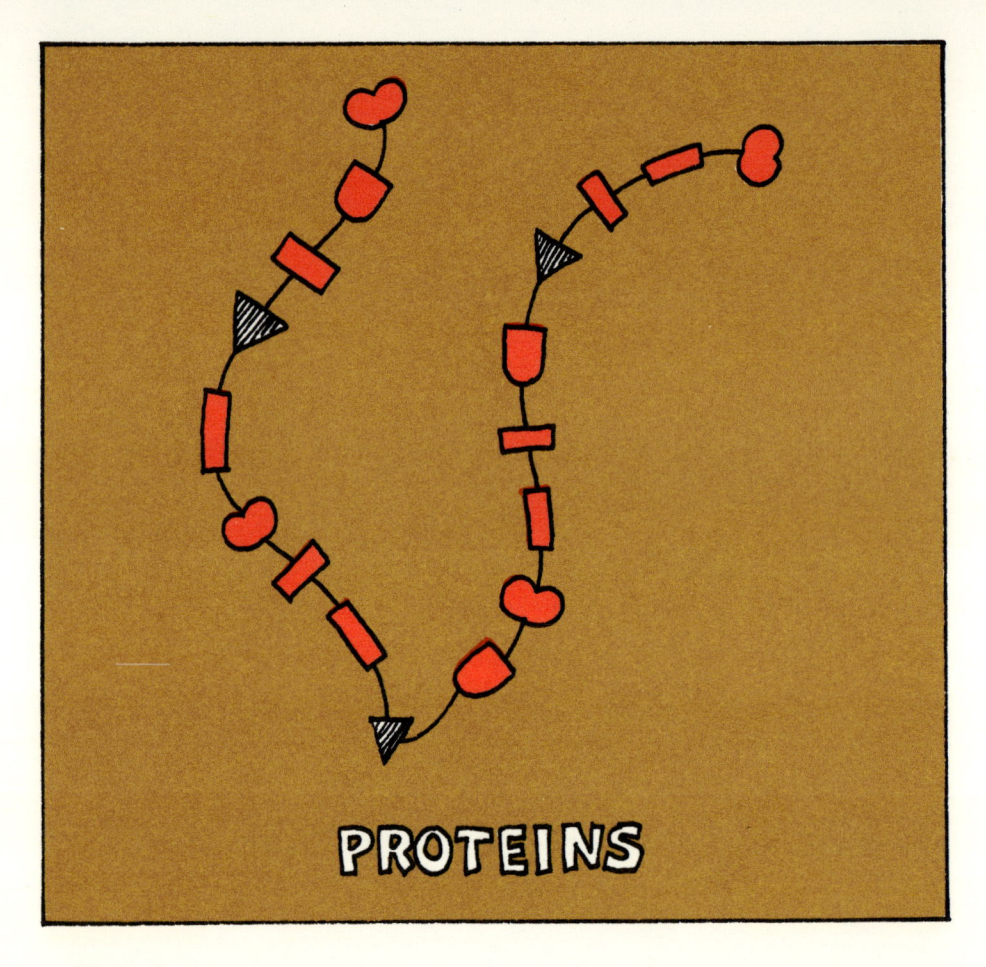

Fats have more energy in them than the same amount of carbohydrates. Large fat particles, like large carbohydrate particles must be broken down into smaller ones before they can be absorbed by the body and turned into energy. The digestion of fat takes longer than the digestion of carbohydrate. Your body is able to store up the digested fat so it can be used for reserve energy.

3. Proteins are made up of long chains of particles called amino acids (uh-MEE-no A-sids). These amino acids are

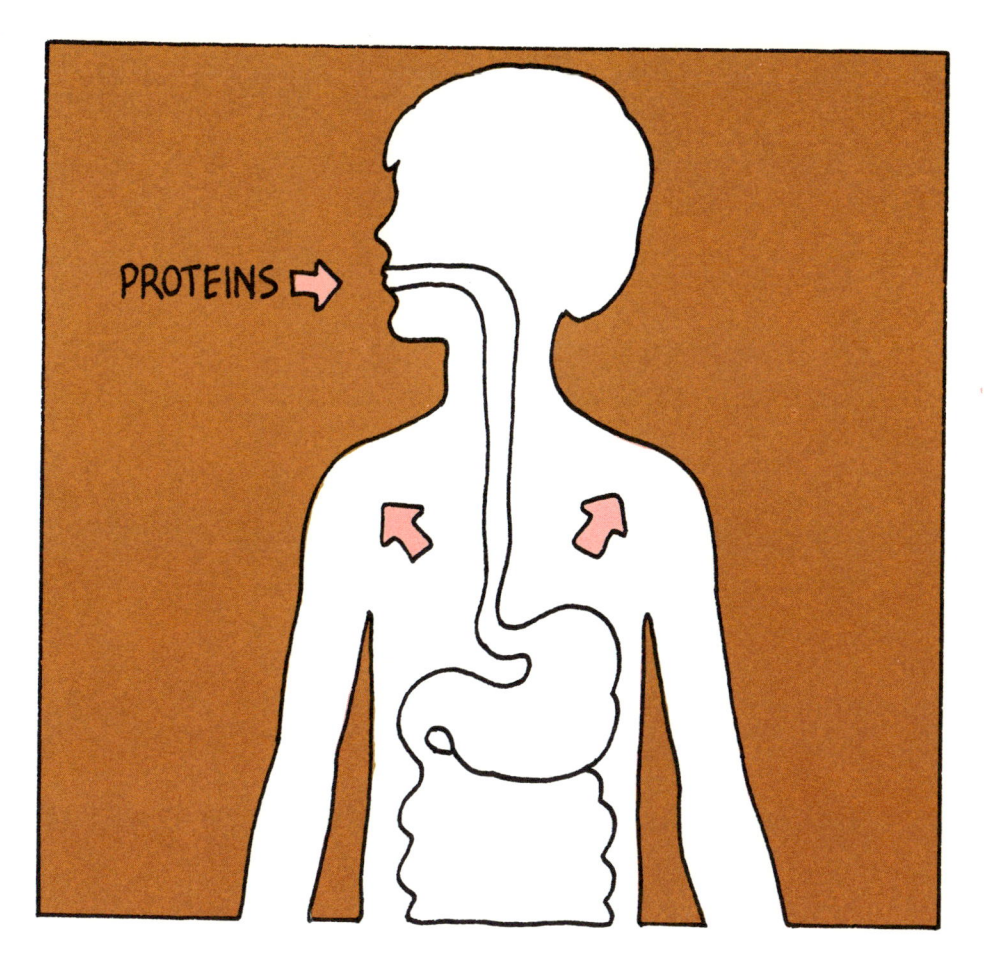

linked together in chains in different combinations and of different lengths. One reason why meat, fish, beans, and cereal taste different from each other is that they all have different types of amino acid chains in them. Another reason is that they have different fats and carbohydrates mixed in with the protein. Like carbohydrates and fats, protein must be broken down into smaller particles by the body before it can be used. The breaking down of protein also takes place during digestion. After the protein has been digested, the amino acids can be used to make energy or to repair worn-out cells all over the body and make it grow.

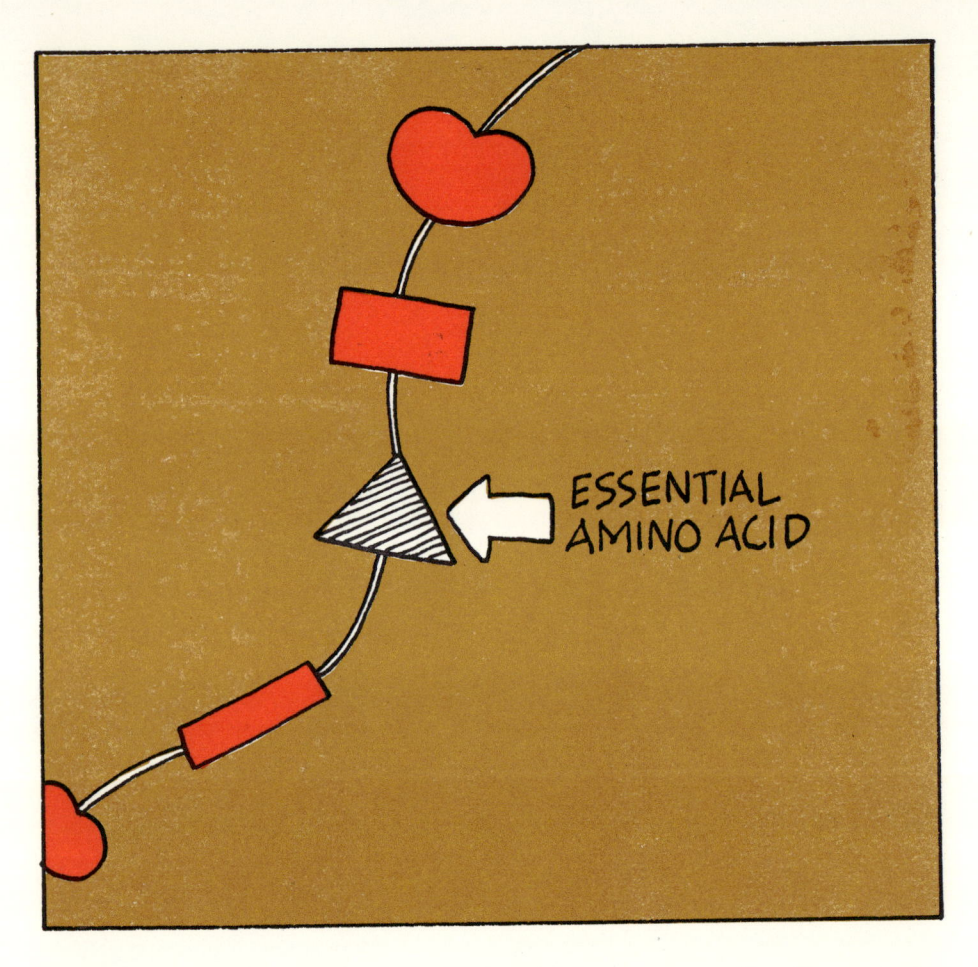

There are some amino acids in proteins which the body cannot make or store. They are called "essential" amino acids. It is important to eat foods that contain essential amino acids often, because they are constantly being used up by the body to make new tissue. Some proteins contain amino acids but not the essential ones. The non-essential amino acids can be used to build some cells and make energy. But without the help of the essential amino acids, they cannot make strong and healthy muscle, skin, bone, hair and blood. If you eat only this kind of protein, you will not be getting the essential amino acids needed to replace your body cells.

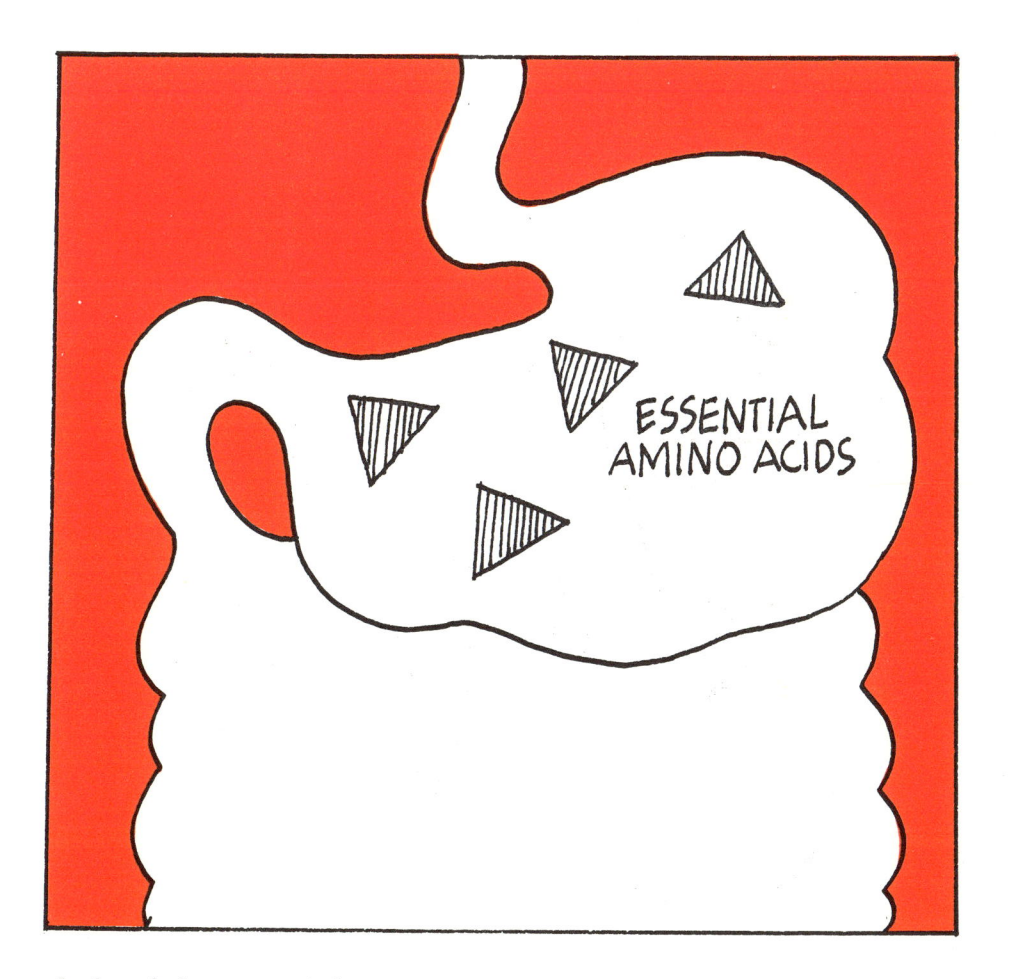

4. Vitamins are tiny particles which are made by certain plants and stored in their leaves, roots, juices, and berries. Certain meats like liver and pork chops also have vitamins stored in them. Some of the common vitamins are named after letters in the alphabet: A, B_1, B_2, B_6, B_{12}, C, D, E, and K. The numbers

after the B vitamins are there to tell them apart. Each vitamin has its own very important purpose in helping the body produce energy and build up its muscle, skin, brain, blood, and bone.

There are many different vitamins in fruits and vegetables. Most of them are well-known, but some were only recently discovered. When an apple or carrot is eaten and digested, the vitamins in it are released and absorbed into the body. Since your body cannot make its own vitamins, and can only store them for a very short time, it is important to renew the supply of vitamins often.

5. Minerals are special particles that are needed by the body often because they are constantly being lost or used up. Salt (sodium chloride) is an example of a mineral that can be lost by the body in sweat and tears. Iron is a mineral that is used in making blood, and calcium and phosphorus are used up in making bone. Over a dozen other minerals are needed by the body, including potassium, sulfur, copper, iodine, cobalt, and

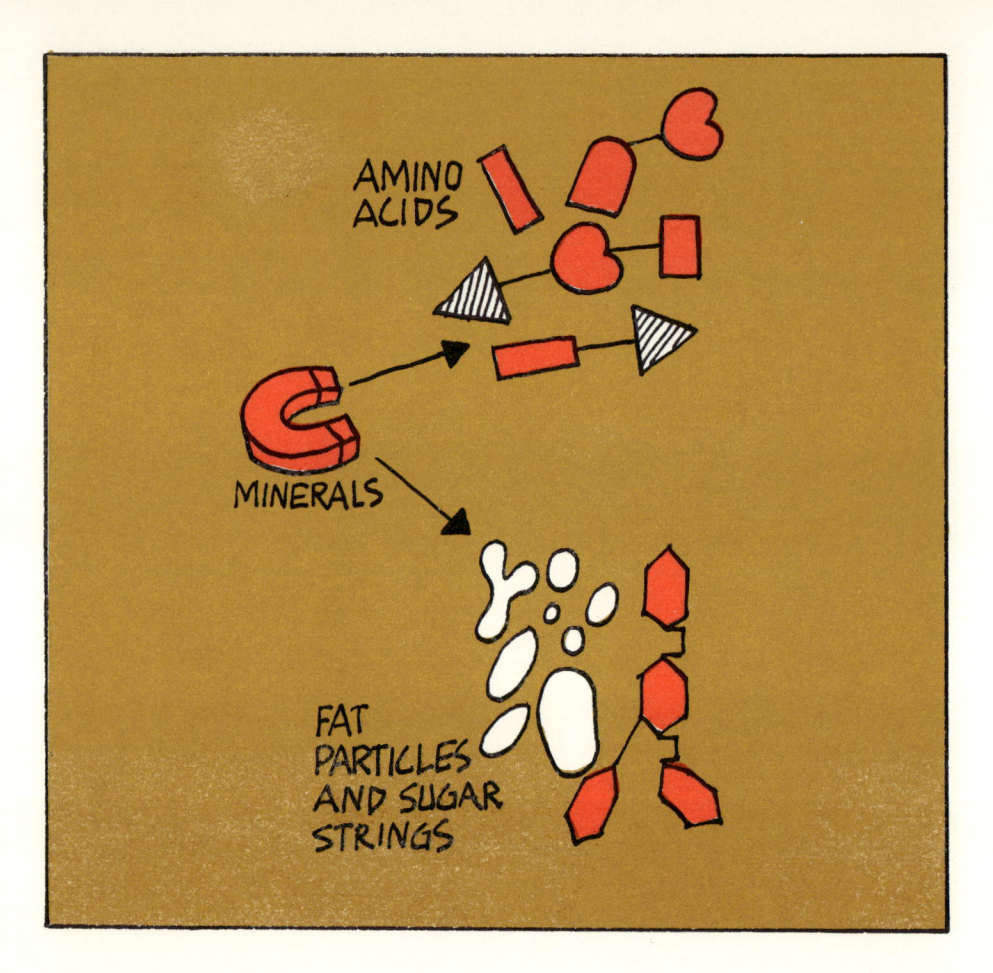

zinc. Many of these minerals are needed in only very small, or trace, amounts. They are used by the body as tiny magnets to attract and hold amino acid chains, sugar strings, and glyceride particles. Various combinations of these nutrients, attached to a particular mineral, form the ingredients needed to make new cells.

  Minerals are usually stored in the plants and meats that you eat. Occasionally, if your body uses a lot of a certain type of mineral, you can take it separately in the form of a pill or syrup to catch up. Sometimes, when athletes sweat a lot, they have to take salt tablets. So a mineral or a vitamin can even be a medicine if you take it in extra amounts to replace big losses by the body.

6. Water is really a mineral. However, because it is so important to every living thing, it is considered a separate nutrient. Water takes part in every stage of breaking down proteins, fats, and carbohydrates into small particles. Water is also needed not only in the digestion of these particles, but also

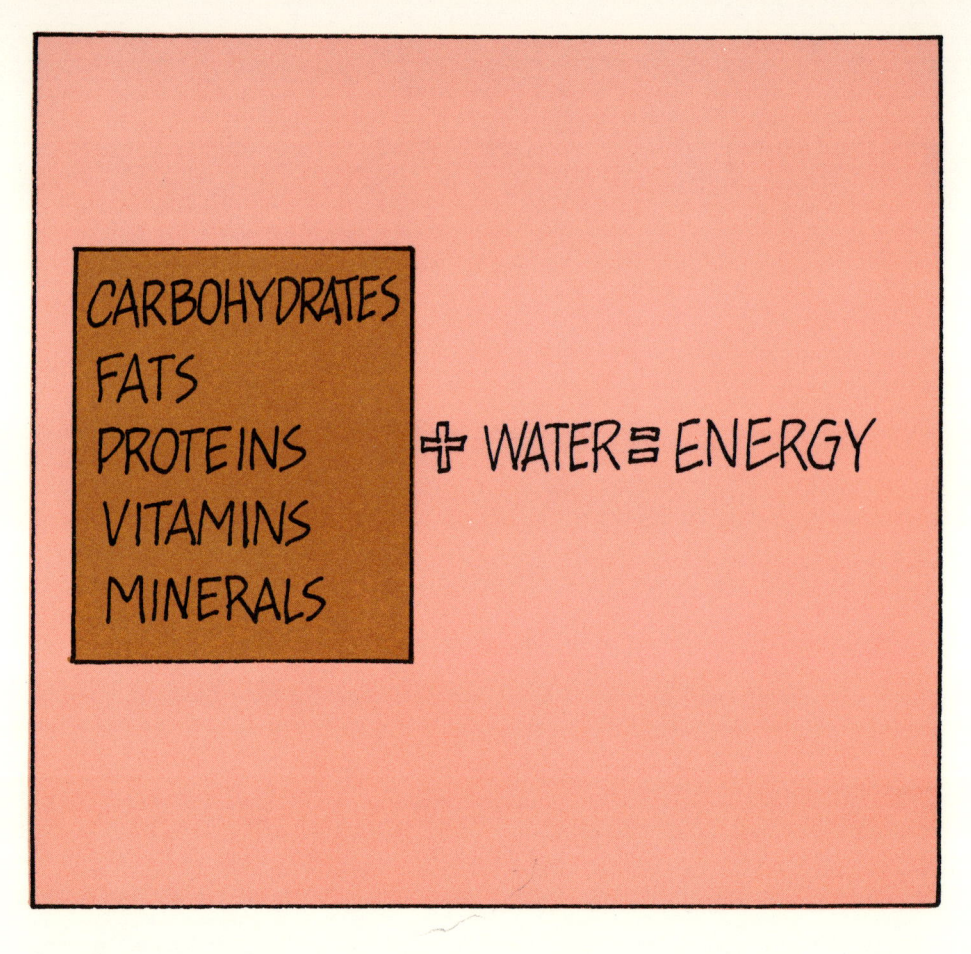

CARBOHYDRATES
FATS
PROTEINS + WATER = ENERGY
VITAMINS
MINERALS

in absorbing them into the body. Water is needed to transform the other five nutrients into energy. It is needed to transform the energy into action or growth. Almost everything you eat or drink has some water in it.

The energy is stored up in food in the form of Calories. Calories are a measure of the amount of stored energy in food that the body can turn into real energy. All food has a certain amount of energy stored in it in the form of carbohydrates, fats, or proteins. Vitamins, minerals, and water do not have any

Calories. So certain nutrients do not have any Calories in them but are still very important. Fats and carbohydrates are nutrients that supply only Calories. If you ate chocolate cake all the time you would be starving your body of the nutrients that prevent sickness. You would be eating only empty Calories.

Chocolate cake is rich in carbohydrates but poor in other nutrients. You could eat nothing but chocolate cake and water for weeks and probably nothing bad would happen to you. However, the cake would be supplying the body with energy and little else. Your reserve supplies of essential amino acids, important glycerides, vitamins, and minerals would slowly be used up. As time would go on, it would be more difficult to make new cells for growth and to protect against disease. You would finally become sick.

The parts of your body which take in food and break it down into its simple nutrients are called the digestive system. When you chew food you break it up into small pieces so that it can be swallowed. Digestion begins in the mouth even before you swallow.

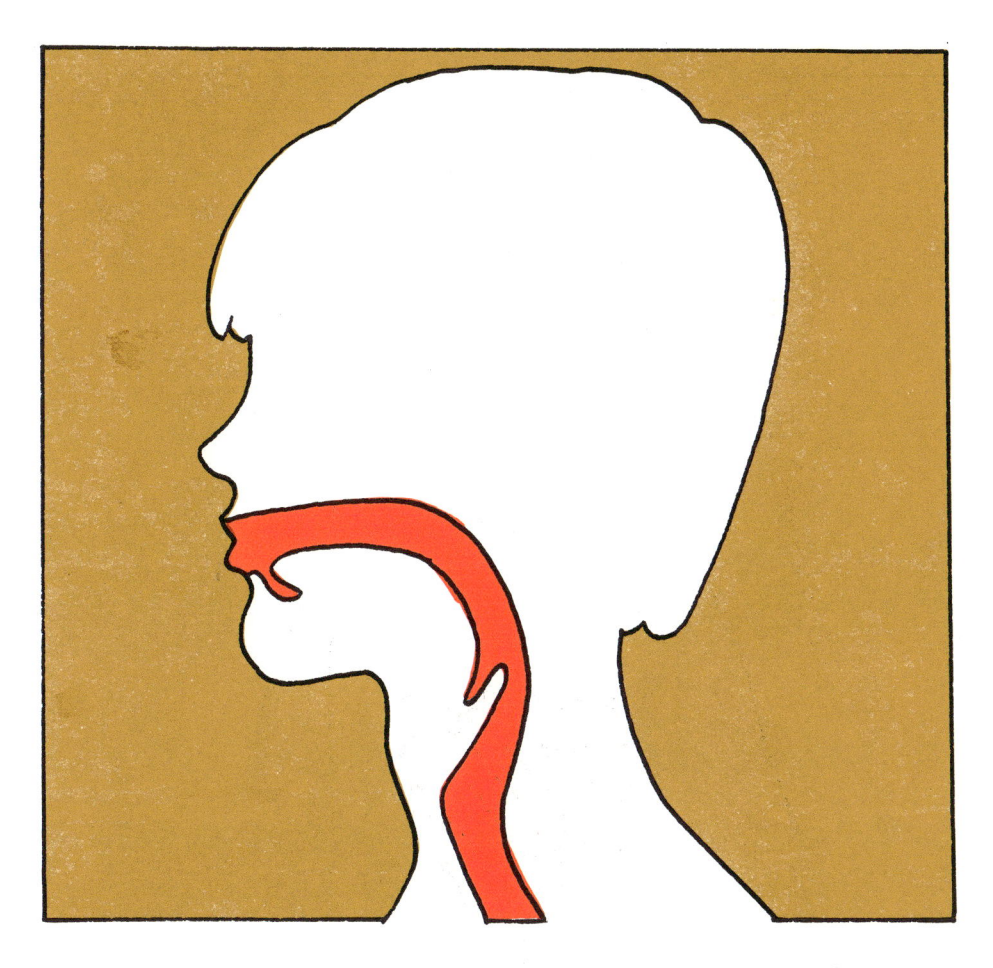

A special fluid called saliva (suh-LIE-vuh) is made inside your mouth. Saliva is rich in enzymes. An enzyme is a substance that helps to break down large particles into small ones. The enzymes in saliva begin to break down the carbohydrates in the food. The very long woven strings of sugar and starch are broken up by this enzyme even before the food passes into the esophagus (ee-SAH-phuh-guss). The esophagus is the tube that carries food from the mouth to the stomach. If you swallow air along with your food, it will come back up the esophagus to your mouth in a burp.

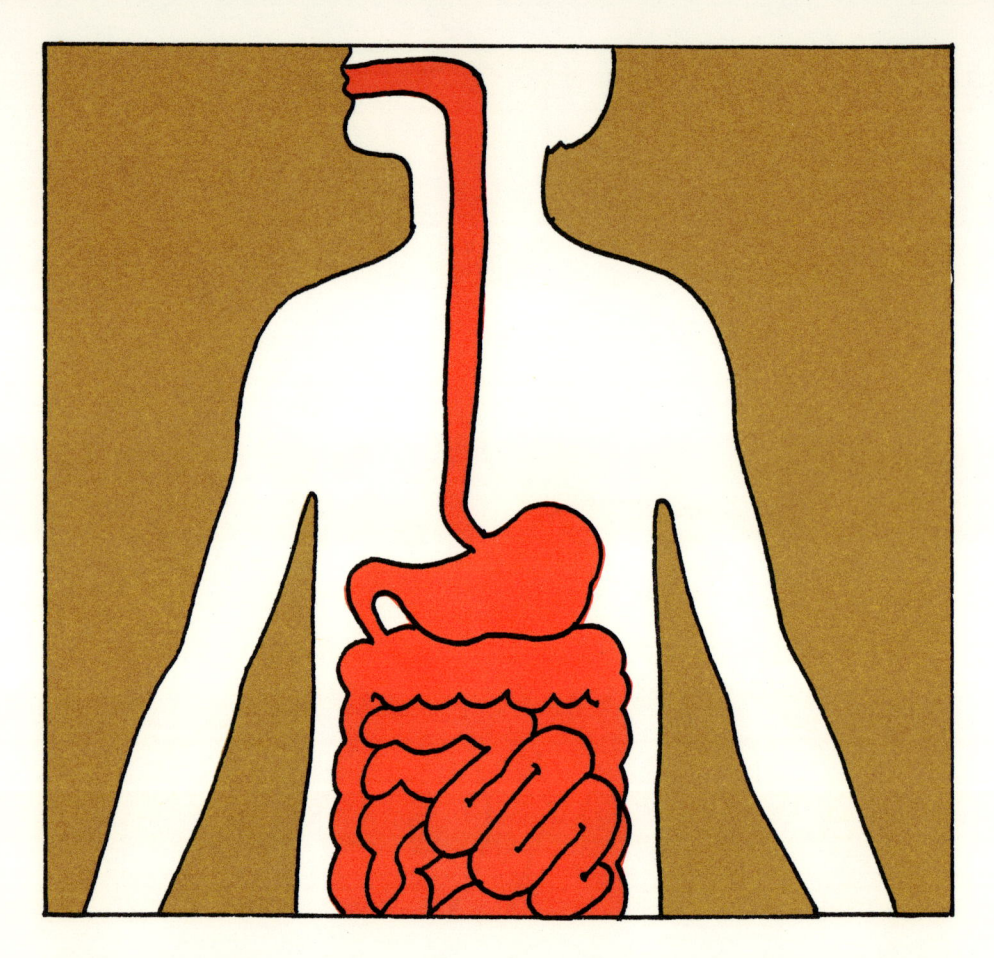

The chewed food arrives in the stomach. The stomach has two important purposes. First, mix the pieces of food together even more. Second, break up the long chains of proteins into shorter chains of amino acids. The stomach does this by making a powerful acid, called hydrochloric acid, which breaks the protein chains at their weak links. The stomach churns and mixes the food in this acid until it turns into a liquid. The stomach can absorb water and some nutrients, but its main jobs are to mix and to hold the food while it breaks down the protein chains.

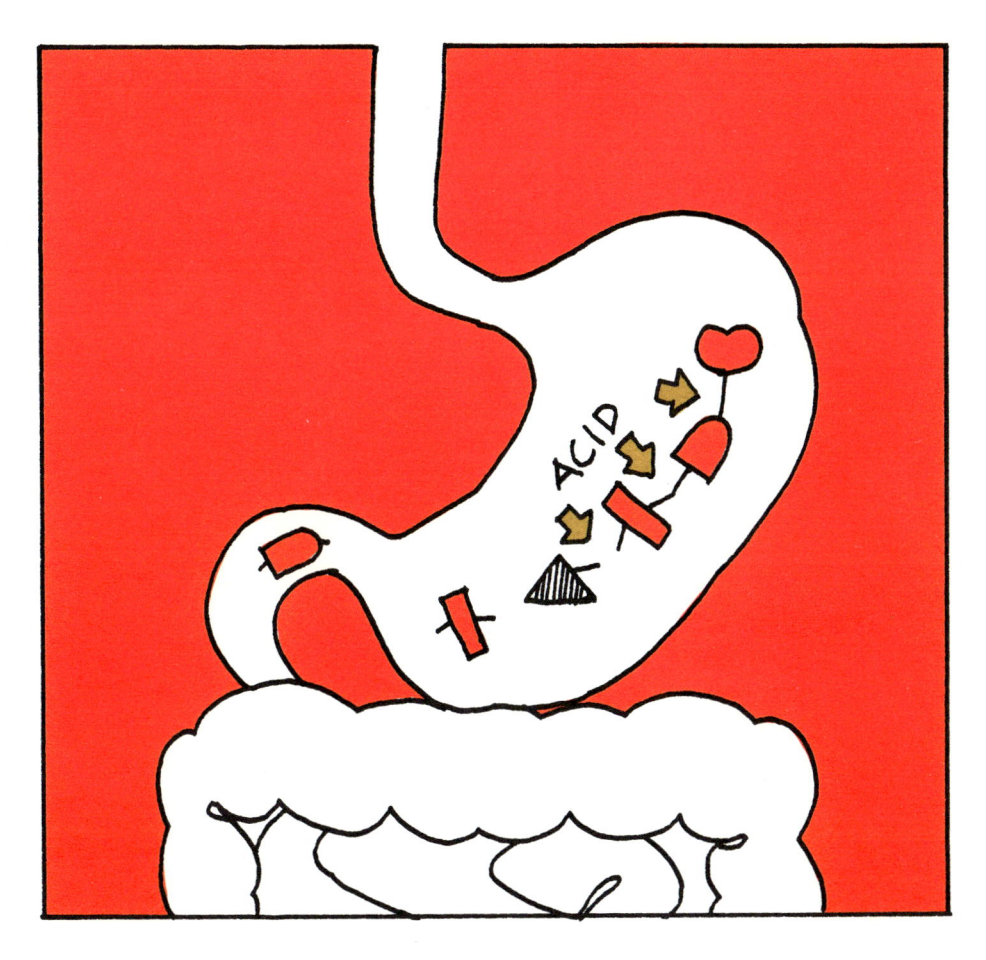

Special muscles make the stomach wall move in the way you might close and open your fist. This squeezing action pushes the liquid food in waves toward the small intestine. The noises you sometimes hear around your stomach are made from the waves moving the food farther along the digestive

SMALL INTESTINE

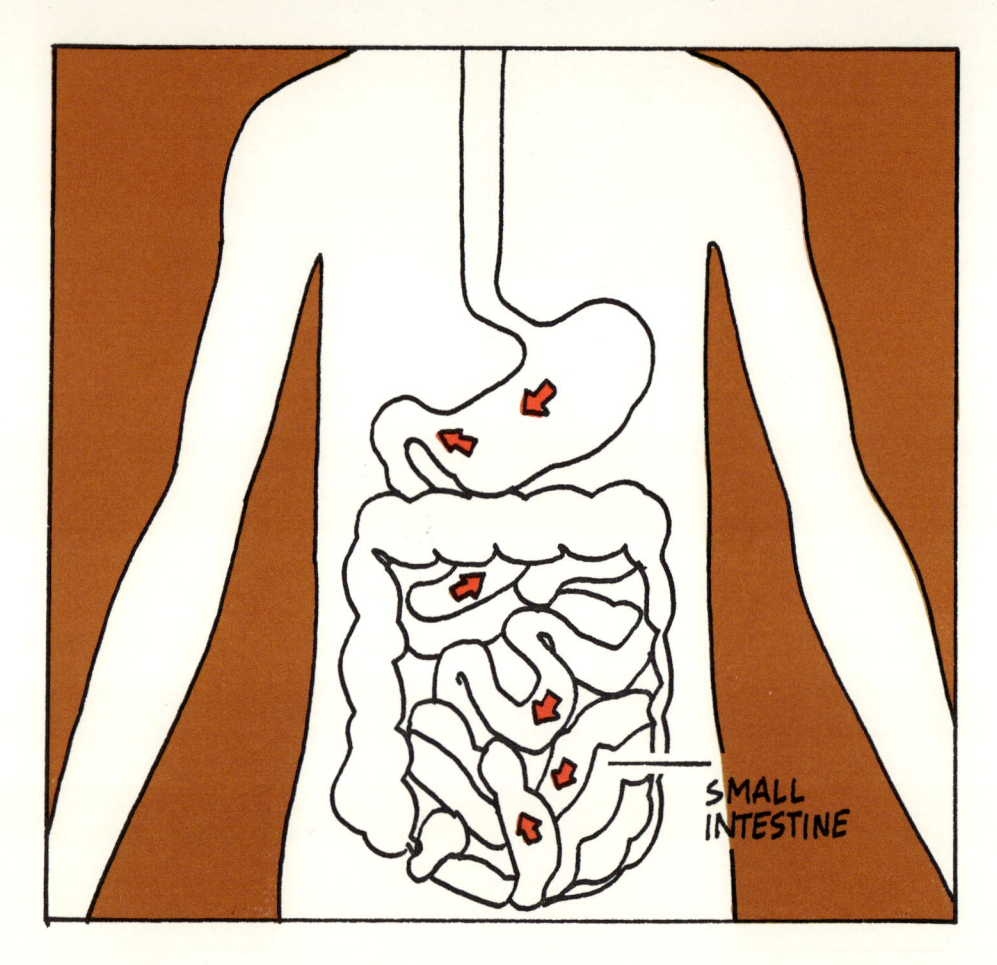

tract. If you eat something spoiled, or become sick, faster and stronger waves may move the food the other way, back up through the esophagus and out the mouth. Vomiting is a way your body can rid itself of food that irritates the stomach or might be bad for you. The sour taste of it is the acid from your stomach.

When the food leaves the stomach it enters the small intestine. The small intestine is a tube over twenty feet long that breaks down food into its basic particles so that they can be absorbed. It is called "small" because it is only as big around as your thumb. The large intestine, which is as big around as your wrist, connects to the other end of the small intestine. It collects parts of the meal that can not be digested or absorbed by the body. The large intestine holds these wastes until they can be eliminated. The large intestine is only about four feet long.

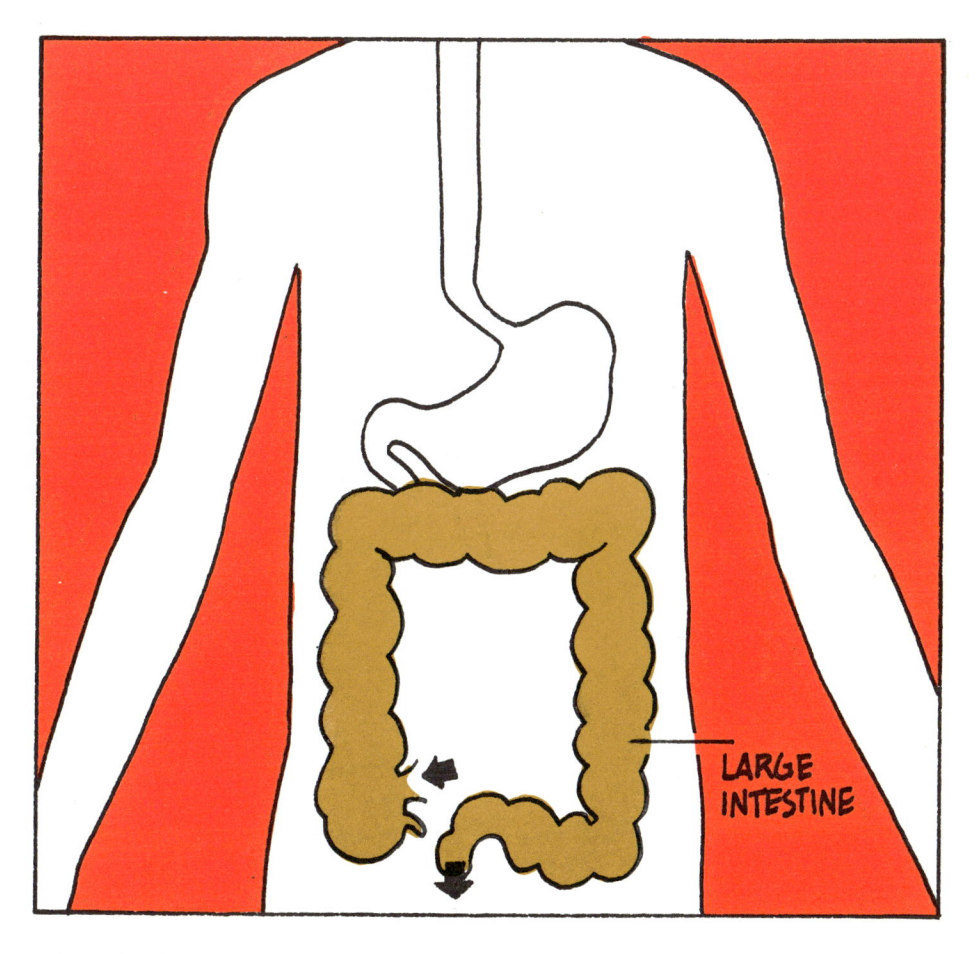

There are special enzymes in the first part of the small intestine. Some of these enzymes continue the work of breaking

PANCREAS

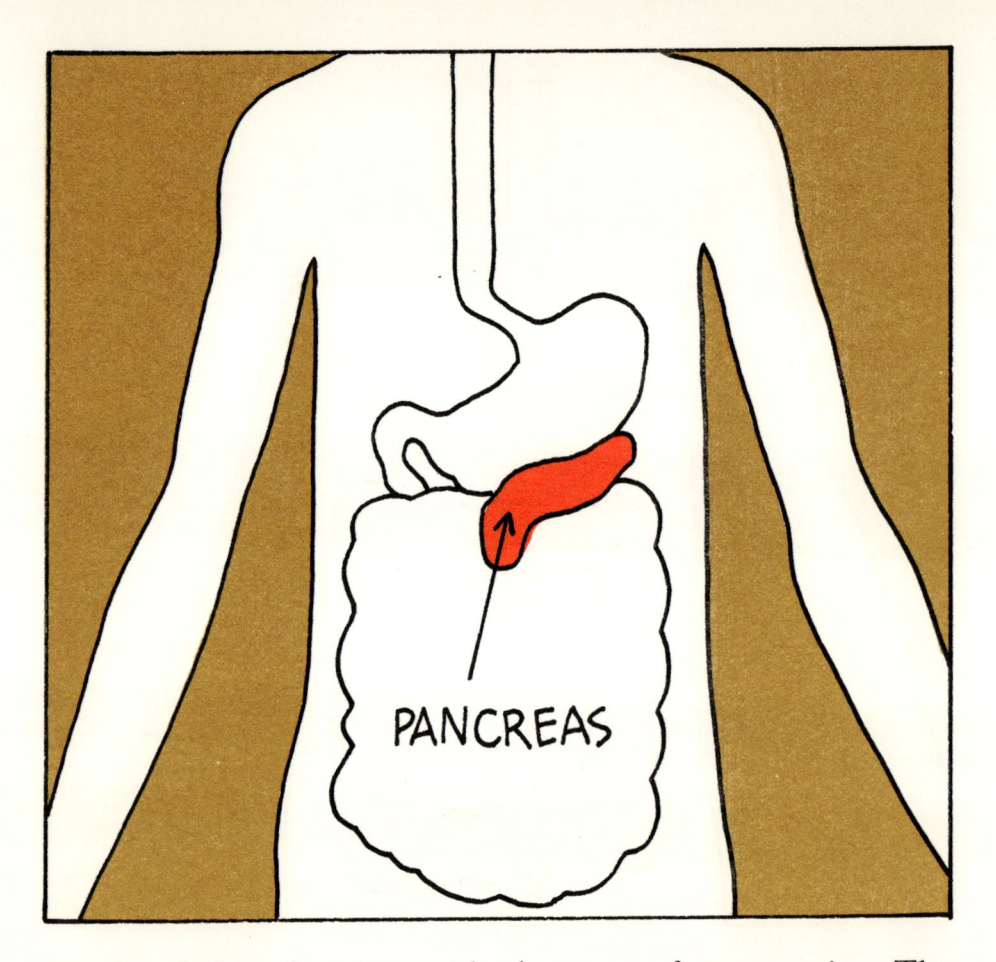

up the chains of amino acids that come from proteins. The enzymes finally break down most of the protein into simple amino acids that can be absorbed into the body. Other enzymes continue the job of breaking down the strings of carbohydrate, which was begun in your mouth. These enzymes finally break down the carbohydrate into simple sugars which can then be absorbed by the body. One of these enzymes is the same enzyme that is in your saliva. It actually is made for the small intestine by another organ right next to it. When the food passes by, this enzyme is squirted into the food to help digest it. The name of this organ is the pancreas (PAN-kree-uss).

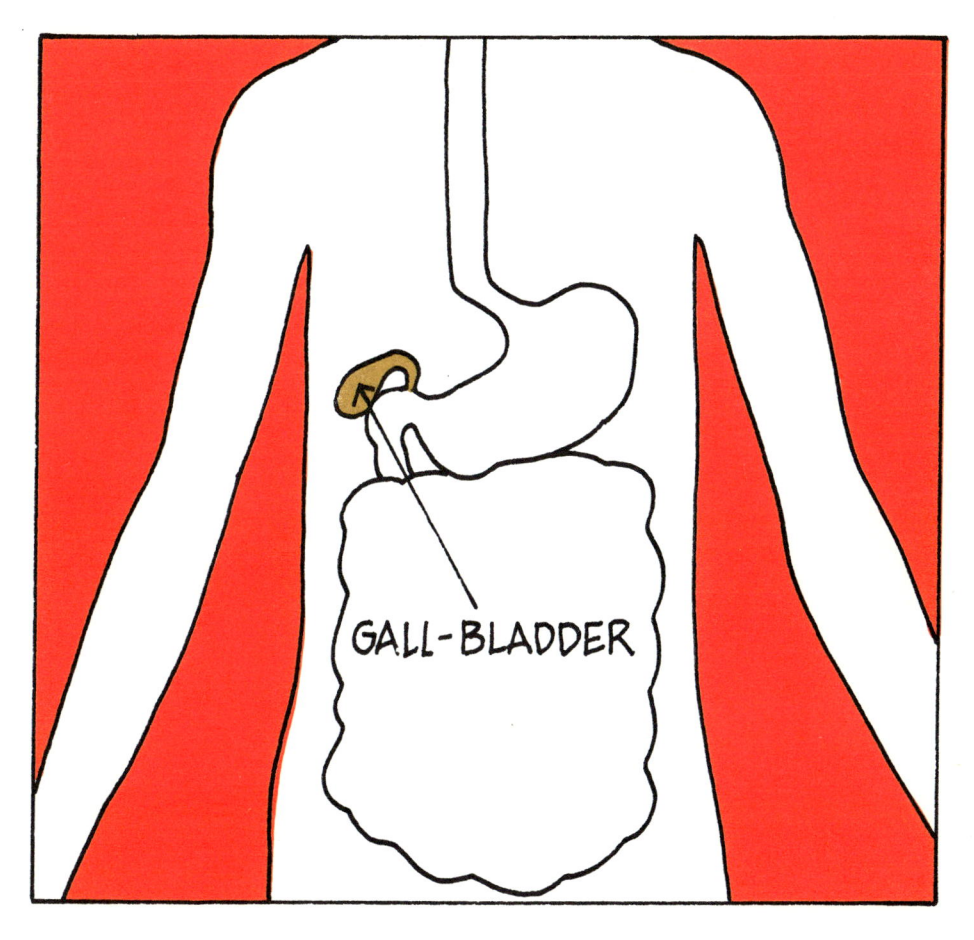

The pancreas makes one other enzyme, too. This enzyme helps to break down fat mixtures into simple glycerides. These small glycerides can then be absorbed by the body.

There is another special organ that helps to digest fat. It is the gallbladder. The gallbladder stores a liquid called bile, which is squirted into the small intestine when food goes by. The bile becomes attached to the fat and breaks it up so that it can mix with the other nutrients and be absorbed.

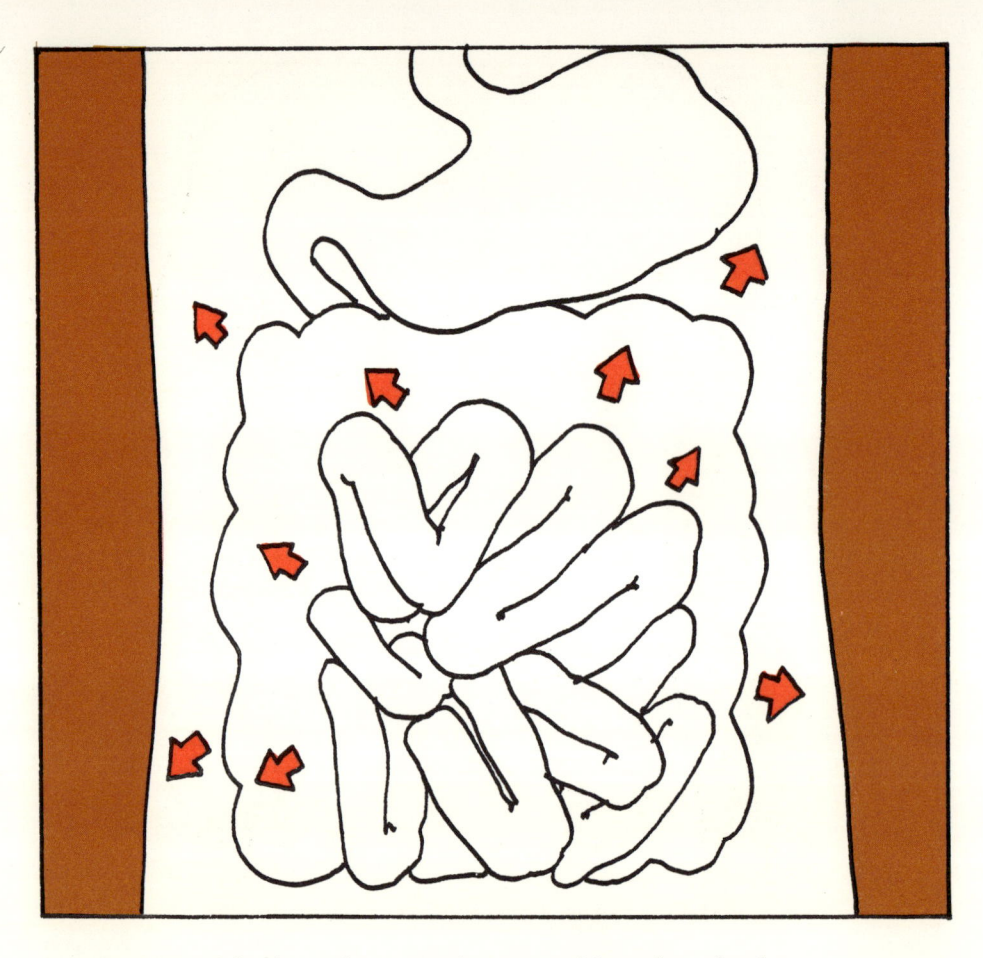

Vitamins, minerals, and water are mixed with the other three nutrients in a piece of food. When the carbohydrates, fats, and proteins are broken down by digestion, the vitamins and minerals are freed. Some vitamins and minerals are absorbed all along the small intestine and some are absorbed at special places in it. For example, water and salt are absorbed along the whole length of the small intestine, while iron and calcium are absorbed at the beginning of the small intestine and Vitamin

VILLI

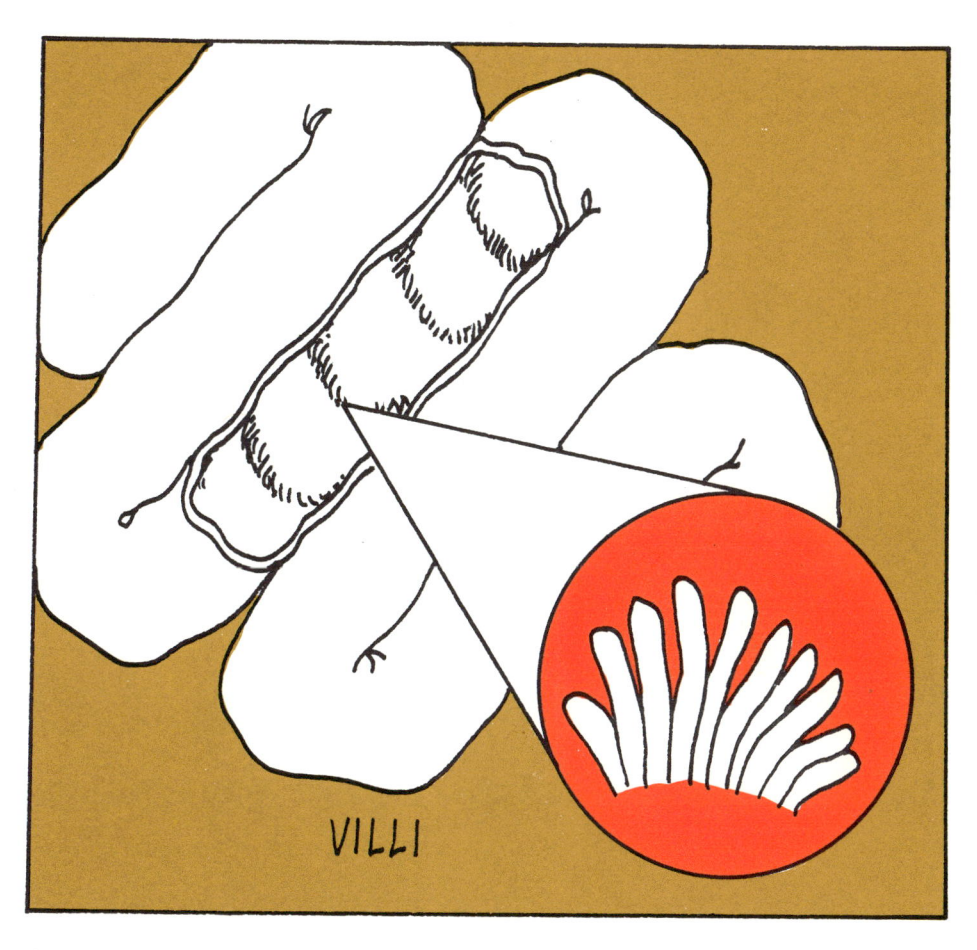

B_{12} is absorbed at its end.

    The small intestine has the special ability to absorb nutrients. Inside its walls are flaps that slow down the flow of liquid food so that the food has more time to be absorbed. The flaps are made up of groups of cells that are shaped like fingers. These finger-like projections are called villi (VILL-eye). Each of the hundreds of cells that make up one of the villi also has very tiny finger-like projections on it called microvilli (MI-krow-VILL-eye). All of these millions of villi and billions of microvilli allow the food to soak in and around them. The villi and microvilli increase the area through which nutrients can be absorbed.

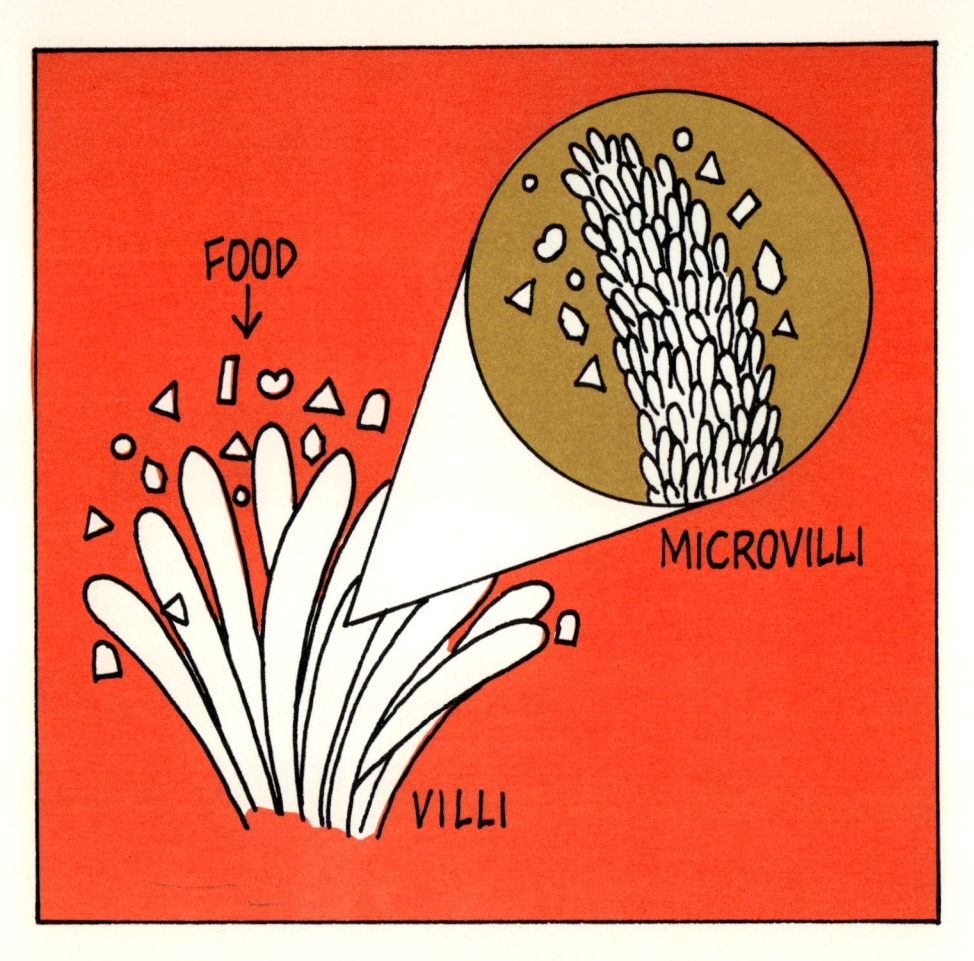

When the nutrient is inside the intestinal wall cells, it is ready to be absorbed into the circulation. Circulation is a word that describes how your blood travels throughout your body. The circulation, or bloodstream, depends on three parts which are connected to one another: the heart, which acts as a pump; the arteries, which act as pipes carrying blood away from the heart when it pumps; and the veins, which act as pipes carrying blood from the distant parts of the body (including the small intestine) to the heart. The villi contain tiny blood vessels which pick up the nutrients. When the nutrients cross from the cells of the villi into the circulation, they become mixed with your blood.

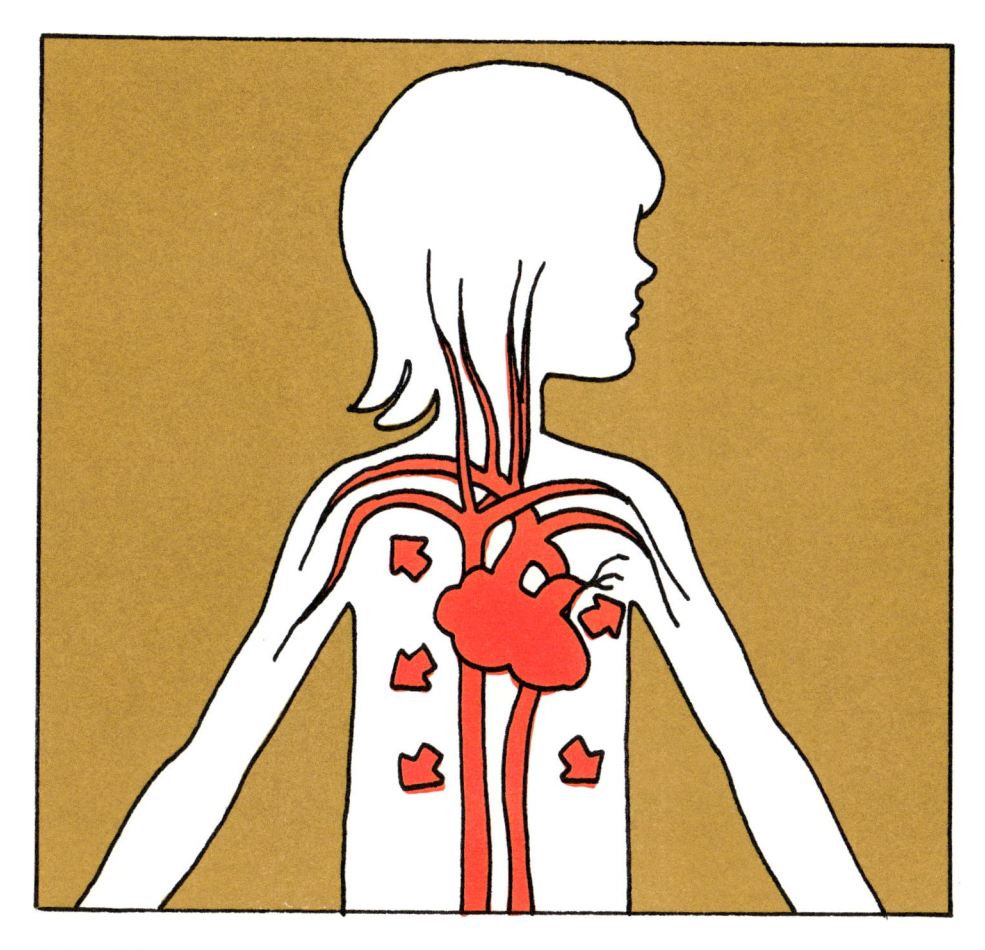

The mixture of different kinds and different amounts of nutrients passes from the cells of the villi into a vein. The vein carries the nutrients mixed with blood toward the heart. Before the nutrients reach the heart, they must pass through a large organ called the liver. The liver filters the blood and nutrients through its channels and keeps the nutrients it needs to do its work.

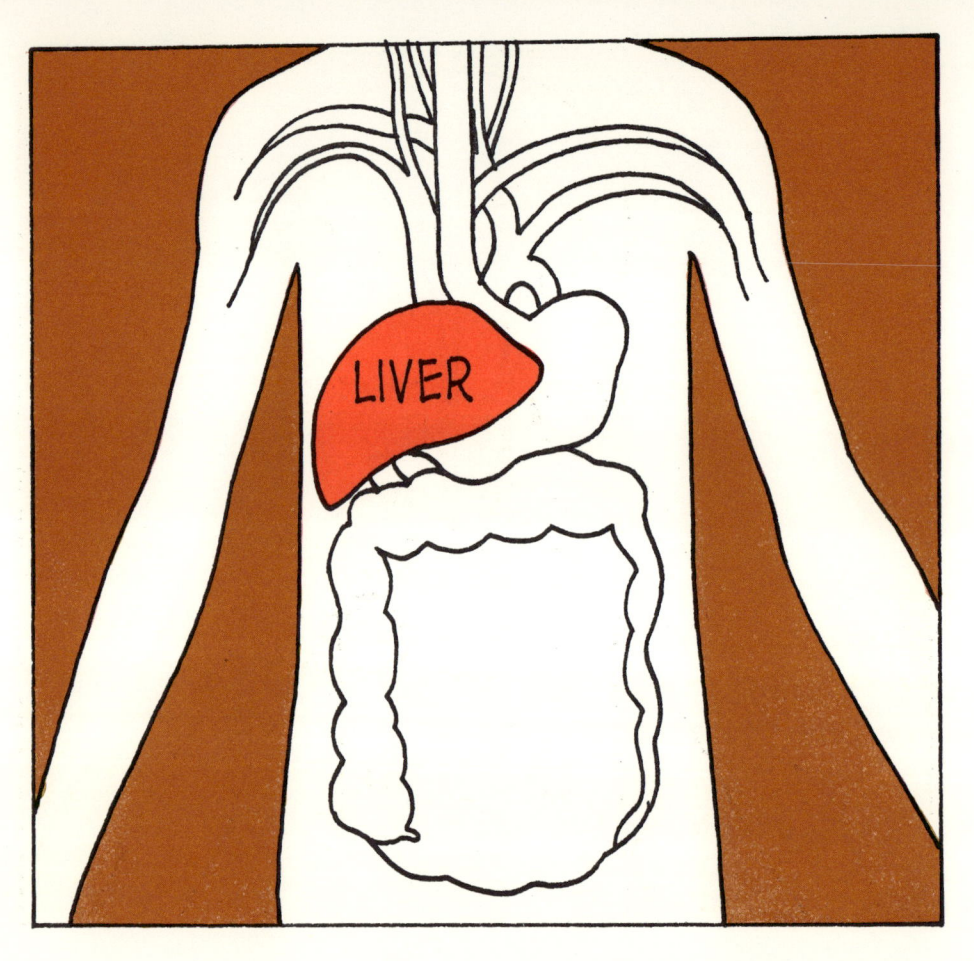

The rest of the nutrients continue in the bloodstream to the heart. The heart pumps the blood which is rich in nutrients to the lungs. In the lungs, the blood takes on oxygen. Oxygen is needed to help transform nutrients into energy. Then the blood, rich in both oxygen and nutrients, returns to the heart.

The heart pumps this blood to every part of the body. Nutrients travel to make the cells that make hair and fingernails grow. Nutrients are turned into quick energy that makes arms and legs move. Nutrients even travel to the stomach, where they are turned into energy which helps the stomach make the waves of food pass to the small intestine.

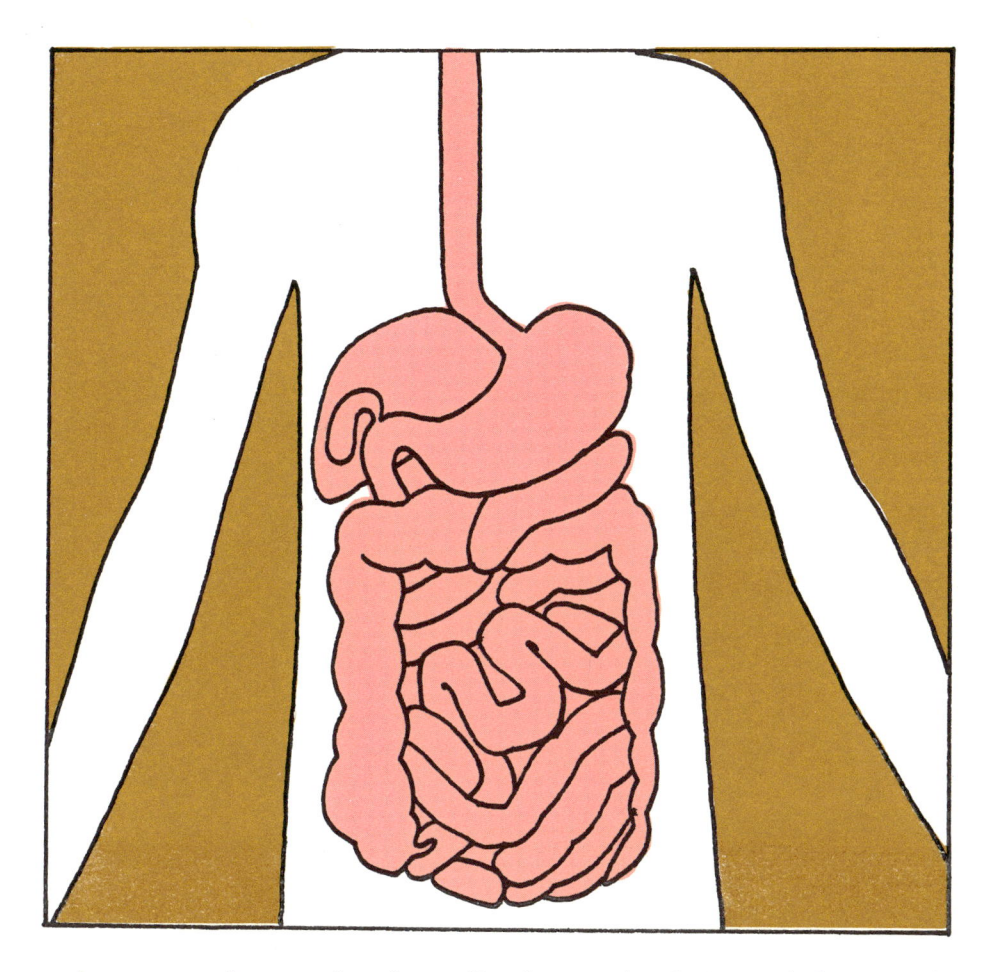

Sugar is used mostly to make quick energy and can be stored by the body in only very small amounts. Amino acids, vitamins, minerals, and water are used by the body to replace worn-out or injured cells, and to make new ones. These nutrients can not be stored in large amounts either. Glycerides are also used by the body to make energy, but only after the sugars are used up. If glycerides are not needed to make energy they are stored by the body until the time when they will be needed. The fat underneath a person's skin is really stored glycerides. Remember, Calories measure the amount of energy stored in food. Any extra Calories a person eats are turned into fat and stored, whether the food is fat, carbohydrate, or protein.

Something will go wrong with the body if it does not get any of the six kinds of nutrients. For example, if a person can not get water he will shrivel up and die. Thirst is a warning from your body that you need water. The feeling of thirst is caused by a special kind of cell in your brain. This kind of cell can tell when the blood lacks water and is too thick. It signals the body and tells it how much water to drink in order to return the blood to its proper water balance. In most parts of the world, water is easy to find. In some parts of the world, however, like deserts, water is as difficult to find as food.

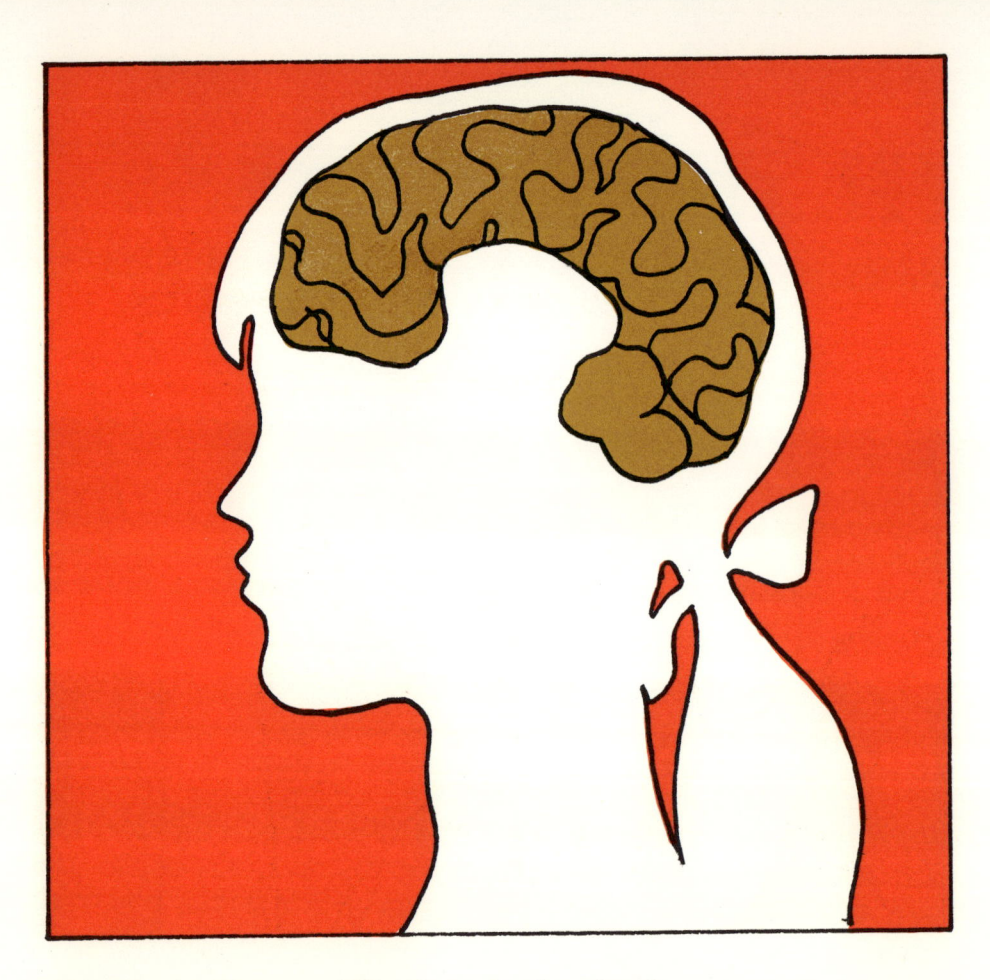

Another special kind of cell in your brain signals you when the level of sugar in your blood is too low. When the level of sugar drops too low you feel nervous and hungry. Hunger is the way your body warns you that you need food. When you digest a meal, sugars, amino acids, and glycerides are absorbed into the circulation. The carbohydrates you eat will raise your blood-sugar level at once. Amino acids and glycerides can also be made into sugars by the liver. So any of the three nutrients that contain Calories can raise the sugar level in the blood to normal. When this happens, the feeling of hunger disappears.

There are no special kinds of cells in your brain to detect when the level of vitamins, minerals, and the essential amino acids are low. For this reason, you could have very low levels of these nutrients and not even know it. You would not even feel hunger or thirst. You could satisfy your hunger eating only chocolate cake while your body was starving for vital nutrients.

Malnutrition is a word that means bad nutrition. A person

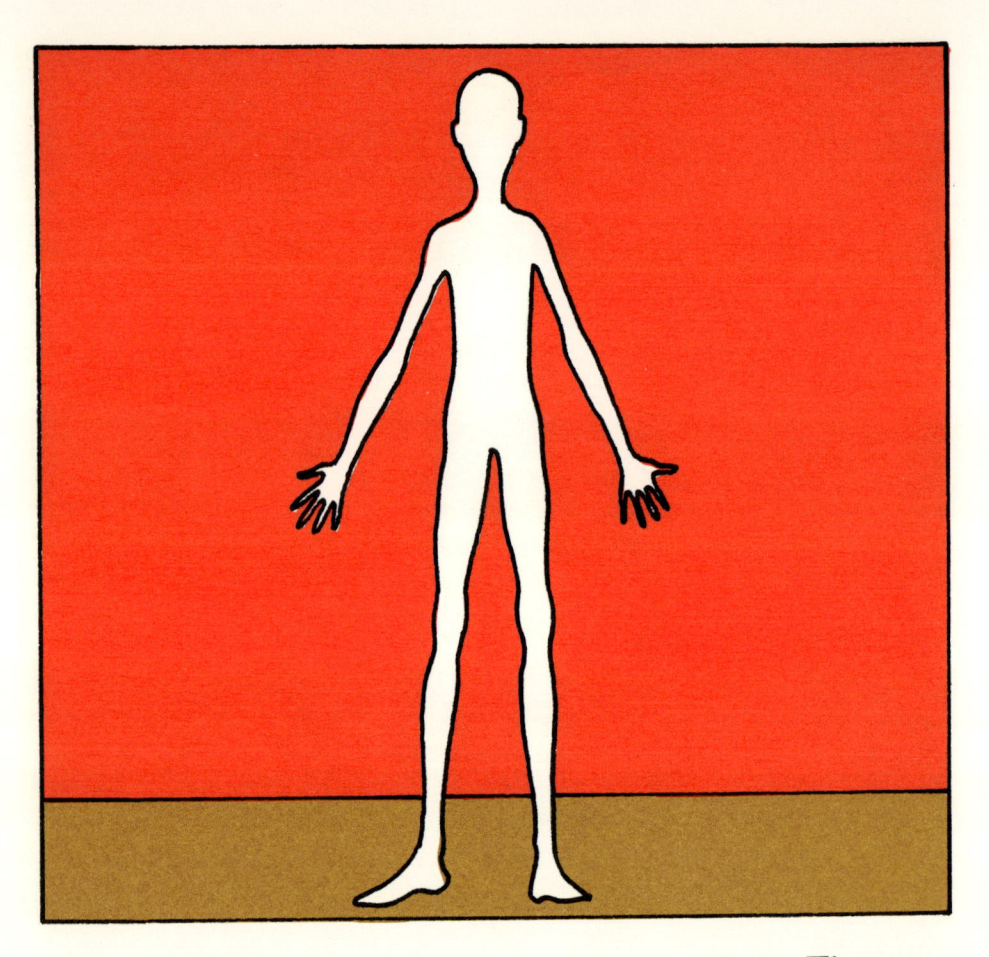

who has malnutrition lacks one or more nutrients. There are different kinds of malnutrition. The worst kind of malnutrition is starvation. In starvation, every kind of nutrient is missing in the diet except water. A person who eats no food soon uses up the small supply of stored carbohydrates. He then uses up the fat he has stored for reserve energy. Finally, if the person does not get any food, he will begin to break down his very own muscle in order to make energy. This is why people who are starving are so thin. Some people who are overweight go on special low-Calorie diets to try to burn up their extra fat. But they must be careful not to use up their proteins, vitamins, minerals, and water.

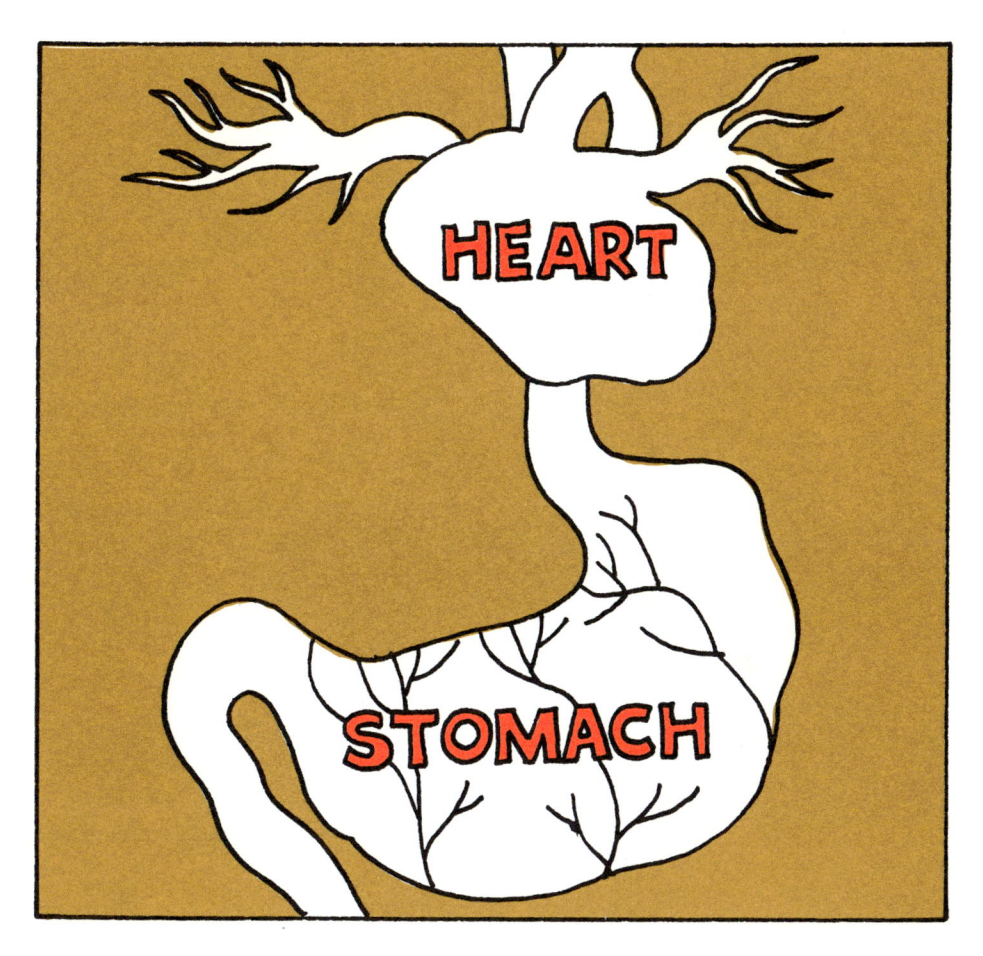

Another kind of malnutrition is called kwashiorkor (KWASH-ee-OR-kor). This is a disease that children get when they do not eat any protein, even though they do eat plenty of carbohydrate and fat. Their hair and skin become faded and dry, because they are not getting protein to make new cells. The heart becomes weak and does not pump blood very well, because it also needs protein to make new cells. Children with kwashiorkor are cross and tired because their brains also need protein to work and develop properly. Yet, even though these childen are lacking in protein, they may not be feeling hunger, because they are eating carbohydrates.

Vitamin and mineral deficiencies are more common than starvation and kwashiorkor. There are many kinds of malnutrition due to different vitamin and mineral deficiencies. The most common mineral deficiency in the world is iron deficiency.

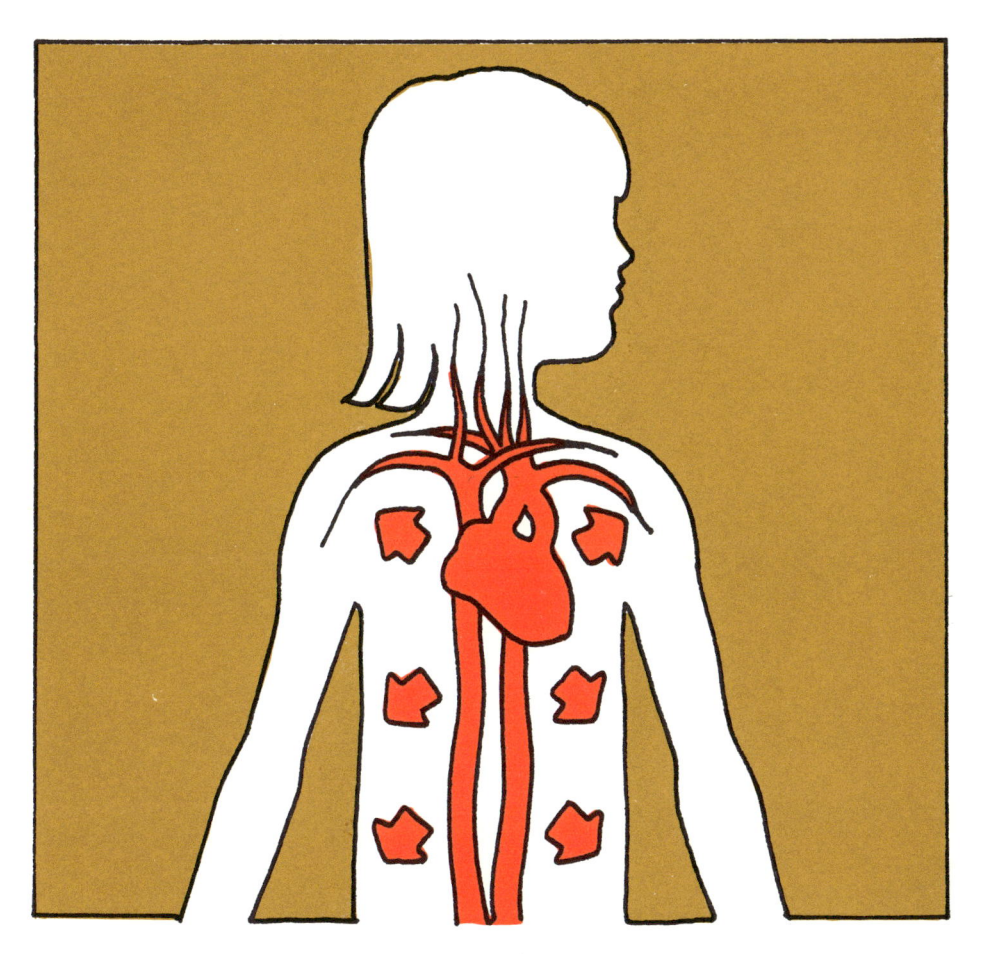

Iron is needed to make the red blood cells that carry oxygen to all parts of the body. If a person's diet is low in iron, a disease called iron deficiency anemia results. Anemia means that there are not enough red blood cells in the body. People with anemia are usually tired, pale, and weak. There are several other causes of anemia, including a lack of vitamins B_6 and B_{12} and of another vitamin called folic acid.

Another kind of malnutrition is that caused by a lack of vitamin C. Vitamin C is needed to keep blood vessels leakproof. When a person's diet lacks vitamin C a disease called scurvy results. In people with scurvy small amounts of blood leak through blood-vessel walls all over the body. When this happens, black and blue marks appear all over the skin and the gums bleed a lot. Scurvy has almost disappeared from the world, because fruits rich in vitamin C are now available to most people.

Eating too much of any one nutrient can also be harmful to the body. Drinking a great amount of water without being thirsty can make a person very sick. Eating too much carbohydrate, protein, or fat can lead to obesity (oh-BEE-suh-tee). Obesity is a disease caused by too much stored fat. The extra fat puts a strain on the body and can make a person weak and tired. Even steak can be bad for you if you eat too much of it. Eating too much of some vitamins and minerals can also be harmful. People can get sick if they take too much vitamin A, K, or D, for instance, or use too much salt on their food.

A balanced diet has the right amounts and the right kinds of nutrients. There are thousands of different food combinations which can make a balanced diet. Too often meals are made up of empty Calories without vitamins, minerals, and essential amino acids. Much of the food you eat contains things which are not nutrients. These are artificial coloring, flavoring, and chemicals which keep the food from spoiling. Just because food looks, smells, and tastes good does not mean that it has the nutrients you need to grow and work. No food is all good or all bad. It depends on how often you eat it, how much of it you eat, and what other foods are also in your diet.

NOTE

These charts are meant to be a starting point for you to find out what nutrients are in various foods. Here are some things to keep in mind when reading this chart:

1. The number of Calories found in a food can vary depending on the size of the serving and the freshness of the food. People between the ages of seven and twelve usually use between 2,000 and 2,500 calories a day, but this, too, can vary depending on age, weight, height, amount of exercise, and general state of health.

2. The percentage by weight of foods is broken down into four nutrients: carbohydrate, fat, protein, and water. The other nutrients (vitamins and minerals) weigh so little they have not been included in the percentages. For example, even though orange juice is rich in vitamin C, less than 1/2,500 of the weight of a glass of orange juice is made up of vitamin C.

3. Since most foods have at least three or four minerals in them, only the more important ones are listed. Certain less important vitamins have also been omitted. The scale for minerals and vitamins is from (1) to (4).

- (1) means present in very small amounts
- (2) present in small amounts
- (3) a fairly good source of this nutrient
- (4) an excellent source of this nutrient

4. Since most meat and fish have all the essential amino acids, a separate listing for this sub-group of nutrients was not made.

Food	Amount	Calories	% Carbo-hydrate	% Fat	% Protein	% Water
Apple	1	80	14	0	1	85
Apple sauce	1 serving	80	19	0	1	80
Bacon	2 slices, cooked	100	1	58	30	11
Baked beans	1 serving	200	22	5	8	65
Banana	1	90	14	2	1	73
Bologna	2-3 slices	80	0	17	16	67

Food	Amount	Calories	% Carbo-hydrate	% Fat	% Protein	% Water
Bread (white, enriched)	2 slices	120	52	4	9	35
Butter	1 square	50	½	83	½	16
Carrots (cooked)	1 serving	35	8½	0	½	91
Catsup	1 tablespoon	15	26	½	1½	72
Cereal (corn, wheat, rice flakes)	1 bowl	100	92	0	5	3
Chicken (not fried)	1 piece with skin	200	0	11	22	67
Chocolate cake	1 slice	400	62	10	3	25
Cod liver oil	1 tablespoon	200	0	100	0	0
Cole slaw	1 serving	60	6	6	1	87
Corn	1 ear or 1 serving	115	20	1	3	76
Crackers	6 average	50	75	10	9	6
Egg	1	75	0	13	14	73
Frankfurter	1 regular	150	2	24	14	60
French fries	10	160	36	16	3	45
Frog's legs	2	70	0	½	17	82½
Hamburger	1 patty	360	0	30	22	48
Honey	1 tablespoon	65	81	0	½	18½
Ice cream	1 scoop vanilla	150	20	13	5	62
Jam/jelly	1 tablespoon	60	70	0	0	30
Lettuce	1-2 leaves	3	4	0	1	95
Liver	1 serving	220	5	8	34	53
Mayonnaise	1 tablespoon	95	1	74	0	25
Milk (whole)	1 8-oz. glass	160	6	4	4	86
Milk (non-fat)	1 8-oz. glass	90	6	½	4	89½
Onion	1-2 slices	10	10	½	1½	88
Orange juice	1 small glass	90	11	0	1	88
Peanut butter	1 tablespoon	90	23	48	27	2
Peas	1 serving	75	17½	½	7	75
Pizza	1 slice plain	180	34	9	10	47
Popcorn with margarine	1 handful	80	43	46	8	3
Pork chops	1 average size	200	0	15	18	67
Potato chips	1 handful or 10 chips	110	51	40	6	3

Food	Amount	Calories	% Carbo-hydrate	% Fat	% Protein	% Water
Prunes (cooked)	1 dish	150	44	0	1	55
Rice (cooked)	1 portion	100	25	0	2	73
Salami	2-3 slices	150	0	38	25	37
Shrimp	6	100	1	1	19	79
Soft drink	1 12-ounce can or bottle	140	10	0	0	90
Spaghetti (without sauce)	1 serving	180	24	½	3	72½
Spinach	1 serving	16	5	½	2½	92
Steak	1 serving ¼ pound	300	0	27	23	50
String beans	1 serving	25	8	½	2½	89
Sugar	1 tablespoon	45	100	0	0	0
Swiss cheese	2-3 slices	200	2	34	29	35
Tomato	2 slices	5	5	0	1	94
Tunafish	1 3½-oz. can	225	0	14	28	58

Food	Minerals	Vitamins
Apple	Calcium (1), potassium (3)	Vitamin C (3), vitamin A (1)
Apple sauce	Calcium (1), potassium (2)	Vitamin C (2), vitamin A (1)
Bacon	Phosphorus (3), calcuim (1)	Niacin (3), vitamin B_1 (4), vitamin B_2 (4)
Baked beans	Calcium (2), iron (3)	Vitamin A (1)
Banana	Potassium (4), magnesium (2), chloride (3)	Vitamin C (2), vitamin A (2), vitamin B_6 (2)
Bologna	Phosphorus (2)	Vitamin B_1 (1), vitamin B_2 (2), niacin (2)
Bread	Calcium (2), phosphorus (2), iron (2)	Vitamin B_1 (3), vitamin B_2 (3), niacin (3)
Butter	Sodium (1), potassium (1)	Vitamin A (3), vitamin D (3)
Carrots	Copper (2)	Vitamin A (4), vitamin C (2), vitamin K (2)
Catsup	Sodium (4)	Vitamin A (3)
Cereal	Minerals and vitamins added in "fortified" brands.	Check box to see amounts.
Chicken	Potassium (2), phosphorus (2)	Vitamin B_2 (3), niacin (4)
Chocolate cake	Calcium (1), sodium (1)	Vitamin A (1)
Cod liver oil	Phosphorus (2), magnesium (3)	Vitamin A (4), vitamin D (4)

Food	Minerals	Vitamins
Cole slaw	Copper (3)	Vitamin C (2), vitamin B$_6$ (2)
Corn	Iron (3), copper (3)	Vitamin C (2), niacin (2), vitamin B$_1$ (2), vitamin B$_2$ (2)
Crackers	Sodium (2), chloride (2)	
Egg	Sulfur (2), copper (3), phosphorus (2)	Vitamin A (1), vitamin B$_{12}$ (3)
Frankfurter	Iron (2)	Vitamin B$_1$ (1), vitamin B$_2$ (1)
French fries	Potassium (3), sodium (2)	Vitamin C (2), niacin (2)
Frog's legs	Phosphorus (2)	
Hamburger	Iron (3), phosphorus (2)	Vitamin B$_2$ (3), niacin (3)
Honey	Potassium (1)	Vitamin C (1)
Ice cream	Calcium (2)	Vitamin A (2)
Jam/jelly	Sodium (1), potassium (1)	Vitamin C (1)
Lettuce	Chloride (2)	Vitamin C (2), vitamin A (2)
Liver	Iron (4), copper (4), sulfur (2), phosphorus (2)	Vitamin C (4), vitamin B$_1$ (4), vitamin B$_2$ (4), vitamin B$_6$ (4), vitamin B$_{12}$ (4)
Mayonnaise	Sodium (4)	Vitamin A (1)
Milk (whole)	Calcium (4), phosphorus (2)	Vitamin A (3) (sometimes fortified with vitamin D. Read label.)
Milk (non-fat)	Calcium (4)	Vitamin A (1) (sometimes fortified with vitamin D. Read label.)
Onion	Potassium (3)	Vitamin C (3)
Orange juice	Potassium (2)	Vitamin C (4), vitamin A (3)
Peanut butter	Potassium (4), magnesium (2), sulfur (4), phosphorus (3), iron (3)	Niacin (4), vitamin B$_1$ (1), vitamin B$_2$ (2)
Peas	Phosphorus (2), iron (2)	Vitamin C (3), vitamin K (3), vitamin B$_1$ (2)
Pizza	Sodium (2), Calcium (1)	Vitamin A (1), vitamin C (1)
Popcorn	Iron (2)	Vitamin A (1)
Pork chops	Potassium (3), phosphorus (3), copper (3)	Vitamin B$_1$ (4), vitamin B$_6$ (2), vitamin B$_2$ (4), niacin (3), vitamin B$_{12}$ (2)
Potato chips	Potassium (3), sodium (2)	
Prunes	Calcium (1), phosphorus (1), iron (3)	Vitamin A (2), niacin (1)
Rice	Iron (2), magnesium (3)	Vitamin B$_1$ (2), vitamin B$_2$ (2)
Salami	Phosphorus (3)	Vitamin B$_1$ (1), vitamin B$_2$ (1)

Food	Minerals	Vitamins
Shrimp	Sulfur (2), iodine (2), copper (3)	Niacin (2)
Soft drink	Sodium (2), chloride (2)	————
Spaghetti (without sauce)	Phosphorus (1)	Niacin (3)
Spinach	Iron (3), potassium (3), chloride (3), magnesium (2)	Vitamin A (4), vitamin B₂ (3), vitamin B₆ (3), vitamin C (4)
Steak	Iron (2), calcium (1), phosphorus (2)	Vitamin B₂ (3), niacin (4)
String beans	Potassium (2)	Vitamin C (3)
Sugar	————	————
Swiss cheese	Calcium (4), phosphorus (3), iron (1)	Vitamin A (4), vitamin B₂ (2), niacin (2)
Tomato	Potassium (4)	Vitamin A (4), vitamin C (2)
Tunafish	Sodium (3), potassium (3), iodine (2), phosphorus (2)	Niacin (3)